TALES FROM

THE CITY STATE

OF

OPHIR
LAND OF OPULENCE

C. Mpumelelo Mängenä

Copyright © 2024

TALES FROM THE CITY STATE OF OPHIR.

C. MPUMELELO MÄNGENÄ.

ALL RIGHTS RESERVED.

The content of this book is the intellectual property of C. Mpumelelo Mängenä; therefore no part of this book may be reproduced, duplicated, or transmitted in either electronicmeans or printed format in any form without the author'swritten permission, except for short quotations used for publishing articles or reviews.

The Version of every scriptural quotation is specified.

Catalog

DEDICATION 5
PROLOGUE 6
FOREWORD 9

ONE 13
    Michael, The Richest Man In Ophir

TWO 23
    Sarah's Legacy Of Wealth

THREE 30
    Connie's Quest For Financial Independence

FOUR 43
    Josiah And The Power Of Persistence

FIVE 51
    Esther's Debt And The Blessing Of UNkulunkulu

SIX 62
    Ethan's Journey To Wealth

SEVEN 69
    Seven Practical Steps To Cure An Empty Bank Account:

EIGHT 72
    David's Secret To Wealth

NINE 80
    Cultivating Good Habits

TEN 84
    Joseph and the Five Laws of Gold

ELEVEN 90
    The Five Laws Of Gold And Practical Applications

TWELVE 95
    Gold

THIRTEEN 101
    Why Is Gold Important?

FOURTEEN **108**
    Why Is Financial Education So Important?

FIFTEEN **112**
    Conclusion and Author's Advice

RECOMMENDED ACTION AND BOOKS TO STUDY **114**

    BOOKS TO STUDY: 117

BIBLICAL RECORDS OF THE LAND OF OPHIR **121**

DEDICATION

To my children,

I found myself pondering, "What knowledge do I possess now that I wish my 12 to 18-year-old self had known?" The answer lies within the pages of this book. "Be fruitful, and multiply, and replenish the earth, and subdue it, and have dominion." This represents the original intent, the very first commandment. Discover your unique niche and purpose, striving to become the best version of yourself. As it is said, "Whatever your hand finds to do, do it with all your might; for there is no work, device, knowledge, or wisdom in the grave, where you are headed."

–Much love, Dad.

PROLOGUE

Ophir is an ancient biblical location mentioned in the Old Testament of the Bible. It was known for its wealth and was often associated with gold and precious stones.

The exact location of Ophir remains uncertain, and there are various theories about its whereabouts. One theory suggests that Ophir was situated on the southeastern coast of Africa, which corresponds to present-day Zimbabwe, Mozambique, and South Africa. This hypothesis is based on descriptions in the Bible and other ancient texts, as well as archaeological findings in the region.

Historically, Southern Africa, particularly Zimbabwe, was renowned for its extensive gold reserves. The Kingdom of Zimbabwe, which flourished between the 11th and 15th centuries, was known for its prosperous gold trade. The Great Zimbabwe Ruins, a UNESCO World Heritage Site, provide evidence of the region's gold mining and trading activities.

During the European colonial era, explorers and traders sought to discover the mythical city of Ophir and its treasures. This search for Ophir was driven by the desire for wealth and the abundant gold in the region. However, the exact connection between the biblical Ophir and the historical gold-producing regions of Southern Africa remains a topic of discussion.

Genesis 2:10-12 ESV

"A river flowed out of Eden to water the garden, and there it divided and became four rivers. The name of the first is the Pishon. It is the one that flowed around the whole land of Havilah, where there is gold. And the gold of that land is good; bdellium and onyx stone are there"

The City State Of Ophir includes extracts from tablets said to have been found at the ruins of old Zimbabwe. It has been translated, expanded, and updated for Kingdom Press by C. Mpumelelo Mangena.

Biblical Records Of The Land Of Ophir: Throughout the mini-series, we see individuals encounter challenges, learn financial lessons, and implement strategies for wealth accumulation based on the principles lived out by men and women of wealth since the dawn of time.

The narratives blend biblical elements with the timeless wisdom of the ages,
providing readers with practical advice for managing their personal finances..

"The silver is Mine, and the gold is Mine," Haggai 2:8 NKJV
SoNini NaNini

FOREWORD

—The wealth of a nation is determined by the individual wealth of its people.‖ When citizens attain and apply knowledge, wisdom, and understanding to create businesses, countries can become prosperous. Let's look at some factors that determine the wealth of individuals and nations:

- **The creation of businesses and division of labor are the foundations of all economies:**

There are a few sectors in an economy. The primary ones are commerce, manufacturing, construction, and services such as health and finance. The list of businesses in these sectors is endless. However, there is a common denominator, which is land. Land ownership and utilization are critical. Therefore, the author urges the reader to have this at the forefront of their mind at all times as they continue to read, study, and grow.

For business owners, the setup is generally the same for efficiency and maximum production objectives. For example, a car manufacturing business with a single employee would be exceedingly slow and tiring.

A better way would be to have different people specialize in specific tasks. This way, they become extremely skilled at what they do, and work gets done faster and better. The business produces crucial capital, and the division of labor creates employment.

Saving and Investing: Saving profits from sales is important because they can be reinvested in things that generate even more income. When people invest wisely, it helps the economy grow and creates more wealth and opportunities for everyone.

- **Natural resources:**

Resources like gold, gems, or oil can kick-start a country's economy and create wealth at an accelerated pace. Education in these fields, good infrastructure, and fair rules and laws contribute to a prosperous country.

- **Free trade:**

Trading with other countries is important. It's similar to exchanging things you have for things you need. When countries have fewer restrictions on trading, it is easier for them to acquire products and services from other nations, which benefits everyone.

- **Role of Government:**

The government's job is to ensure everyone plays fair and follows the rules. It's also important for the government to protect people and keep them safe. But excessive government control can hinder progress and limit people's potential.

Overall, when people are free to pursue their own interests and use their skills, and when countries trade with each other openly, it leads to more prosperity and a better life for everyone.

This is just a simplified summary of individual and national wealth building, which is hoped to inspire the reader to further their knowledge, wisdom, and understanding of wealth creation.

> —Business is a good idea because it's a God idea. -
> **Myron Golden**

THE CITY STATE OF OPHIR

ONE

Michael, The Richest Man In Ophir

Once upon a time, a young, aspiring merchant named Michael lived in the prosperous city of Ophir. Like many other young men his age,
Michael was trapped in a cycle of financial struggles and unfulfillled dreams. He yearned for a better life, but his meager income and mounting debts seemed insurmountable.

One fateful day, as Michael wandered through the bustling streets of Ophir, he stumbled upon a gathering of wise elders who shared their wisdom on wealth and success. Intrigued, Michael listened intently to their stories and advice, hoping to escape his dire circumstances.

Among the wise elders was a seasoned entrepreneur named Seth, known for his prosperity and generosity. Impressed by Michael's eagerness to learn, Seth took him under his wing, becoming his mentor and guide on the path to financial independence.

Seth's lavish mansion, adorned with riches and fine craftsmanship from across the land, was a testament to his achievements. He was known not only for his wealth but also for his astute approach to risk in the world of trade. His knowledge extended beyond the bustling marketplaces; it reached into the heart of Ophir's financial district.

Under Seth's tutelage, Michael would discover the fundamental principles of building wealth. He would learn the importance of setting financial goals, budgeting, and living within his means.

One day, as Seth was at the docks overseeing a shipment of exotic goods from a distant land, he noticed his young friend, Michael, approaching. Michael was a skilled carpenter, known for his meticulous craftsmanship and intricate woodworking. He had a reputation for creating furniture that was both functional and a work of art.

Michael had come to Seth with a question that had been burning in his mind. "Seth," he began, "I've been pondering the decisions I make in my carpentry work. How do you determine when it's worth taking risks, especially when it comes to business decisions?"

Seth paused, his gaze shifting from the bustling activity of the goods being unloaded to Michael's earnest expression.

"Ah, Michael, you've touched upon an essential aspect of life—a concept that extends far beyond the realm of trade.

Risk appetite is a principle that governs not just commerce but every decision we make."

Intrigued, Michael leaned in, ready to absorb the wisdom his friend was about to share.

Seth continued, "Consider each project we undertake as a piece of furniture. The simplest projects are like stools—the ones we can craft with ease and predictability. They carry little risk because we've honed our skills through repetition. But the true artistry lies in crafting intricate cabinets—complex projects, each unique in design and thus carrying more substantial risks. A single mistake can mar the beauty and functionality of the piece."

Michael nodded, starting to grasp the analogy.

"But," Seth emphasized, "the key is to assess the balance between potential rewards and risks. Ask yourself: What can we gain from this project? Is it an opportunity that could elevate our reputation and craftsmanship? Does it challenge us to grow and learn?"

Michael listened attentively, absorbing Seth's words.

"However," Seth cautioned, "equally important is weighing the risks. Do we have the skills and knowledge to handle the challenges this project presents? Do we have the necessary resources and time? Can we mitigate potential setbacks?"

Their conversations about risk appetite became part of their regular interactions. Seth shared stories of past business decisions, some that had brought great success and others that had been humbling experiences. Michael began to understand that risk appetite was not just about diving headfirst into the unknown but making calculated decisions that could shape their futures.

One day, an opportunity arose that would challenge their understanding of risk appetite. It was an investment opportunity in a fledgling furniture company with immense potential and substantial risks. The allure of potential wealth and the chance to elevate their craft were undeniable.

Seth and Michael sat down to discuss the opportunity. Michael looked at his friend, his eyes filled with anticipation. "Seth, what do you think? Is this the kind of investment we should consider, despite its risks?"

Seth leaned back in his chair, his gaze fixed on the intricate wooden furniture that adorned his mansion. "Michael, this opportunity is like a cabinet of destiny. It offers the promise of great rewards, but it also carries substantial risks. It challenges us to make a decision based on our risk appetite."

They deliberated for hours, carefully weighing the potential rewards against the risks. They considered their financial resources, the state of the market, and the expertise required. Finally, Seth said, "We will invest in this opportunity, but with a clear understanding of the risks involved. We will diversify our portfolio, seek advice from experts when needed, and ensure that we have safeguards in place to mitigate potential setbacks."

Months passed, and their investment in the furniture company proved to be a rewarding decision. The company flourished, and their wealth grew exponentially. Their reputation as astute investors and skilled craftsmen soared, drawing admiration and respect from all corners of the city.

As they stood before the exquisite wooden pieces they had crafted and the thriving furniture company they had invested in, Michael looked at Seth with gratitude. "Seth, it was a risk worth taking."

Seth nodded with a satisfied smile on his face. "Indeed, Michael. Remember, risk appetite is not just about the investments we make but also the decisions we make in life. It's about finding the right balance between ambition and caution. These pieces of furniture and our flourishing investments are a testament to the artistry that blooms when risk is embraced with wisdom."

With each passing day, Michael saved a portion of his earnings, gradually building a foundation of financial stability.

As his savings grew, Seth taught Michael the art of investing. He introduced him to the world of precious metals, exports, and real estate, emphasizing the need for patience and careful analysis. Michael eagerly absorbed the knowledge, studying market trends and seeking out profitable opportunities.

As Michael's experience grew, Seth decided it was time to introduce him to a new level of investment and adventure. They embarked on a journey to distant lands, exploring uncharted territories and delving into the world of high-risk, high-reward opportunities.

Their first stop was the bustling city of Axum, north of Ophir, known for its vibrant trade and diverse marketplaces. Seth guided Michael through the intricacies of investing in precious metals, teaching him the art of assessing market trends and understanding supply and demand dynamics. They spent days immersing themselves in the world of gold, silver, and gemstones, meeting with local traders, and learning about the intricacies of the precious metals trade.

They returned to Ophir with their newfound knowledge and sailed up the eastern coast of Ethiopia with a cargo of exquisitely crafted furniture that Michael had made. The journey was not without its challenges. They encountered treacherous rapids, intense heat, and unexpected delays. However, Michael's skills as a carpenter proved invaluable, as he made crucial repairs to their vessel, ensuring their safe passage. Arriving in the ancient city of Meroe, Michael established connections with local merchants and expanded his export business. His furniture gained a reputation for its exquisite craftsmanship, attracting buyers from far and wide. Word of his unique offerings spread, and soon Michael found himself not only exporting up the Nile but also to India, a land renowned for its rich traditions and love for intricate designs.

The vibrant tapestries, flavorful spices, and opulent textiles in India mesmerized Michael and Seth. Recognizing an opportunity, they dove into importing these coveted goods back to Ophir. They established strong relationships with local artisans and traders, carefully selecting the finest fabrics and spices to bring back to their homeland. Michael's eye for quality and understanding of market demand allowed them to create a profitable import business.

With each passing year, Michael's wealth began to flourish. By buying ships and sailing to faraway lands in search of new markets, he expanded his ventures and diversified his portfolio, ensuring a steady stream of income. His reputation as a shrewd investor and a wise entrepreneur spread throughout Ophir, inspiring others to take charge of their financial destinies.

Michael was now the richest man in Ophir. His journey, however, didn't stop with personal success. He felt a deep sense of gratitude towards Seth and the wise elders who had transformed his life. In a gesture of appreciation, Michael established an educational institution in Ophir dedicated to teaching financial literacy and entrepreneurship to the youth of the city.

The institution became a beacon of hope for aspiring individuals, offering them the tools and knowledge necessary to break free from the chains of financial struggles. With his wealth and experience, Michael served as a mentor and guide to the students, nurturing their talents and igniting their entrepreneurial spirits.

Years turned into decades, and Ophir transformed into a city known for its abundant gold as well as its culture of financial empowerment. Michael's legacy resonated through the generations as his teachings and principles were passed

down from one aspiring entrepreneur to another.

And so, as parents tucked their children into bed at night, they whispered the tale of Michael and his adventures—the visionary carpenter who turned his life around through perseverance and wise financial choices. The children's dreams were filled with visions of a future where they, too, could build their paths to prosperity and success.

In the magical city of Ophir, where dreams come true, the tale of Michael served as a timeless reminder that with knowledge, determination, and the guidance of wise mentors, anyone could overcome adversity and create a life of abundance.

As the stars twinkled in the night sky, the children drifted off to sleep, inspired by the possibilities that lay ahead.

> —Gold and silver are the only true money. All else is credit.‖ - J.P. Morgan

TWO

Sarah's Legacy Of Wealth

In the prosperous city of Ophir, where the golden sun's rays kissed the bustling streets, lived a remarkable woman named Sarah. She possessed a spirit as radiant as the city itself and an unwavering determination to create a legacy of wealth for herself and her family.

Sarah came from a humble background, born into a family of artists in Ophir. As a young girl, she marveled at the vibrant marketplace and dreamed of a life filled with abundance and prosperity. With every stroke of her father's brush and every intricate design she observed, a seed of ambition took root within her.

Determined to chart her own path to financial independence, Sarah embarked on a journey of self-discovery and learning. She sought wisdom from the wise elders of Ophir, studying their teachings and imbibing their insights on wealth and creation.

Sarah recognized that true wealth extended beyond mere material possessions—it encompassed knowledge, integrity, and a commitment to creating opportunities for others.

As Sarah grew older, her entrepreneurial spirit blossomed. She honed her skills in negotiation, mastering the art of spotting opportunities amidst the ebbs and flows of the market. Sarah sought out mentors, wise traders, and merchants who shared their secrets of success, nurturing her understanding of commerce and investing.

One day, while attending a gathering of merchants, Sarah's eyes fell upon a man named Isaac. He exuded a quiet confidence, his words resonating with wisdom. Intrigued by his presence, Sarah started a conversation about their shared passion for wealth creation, forging a connection between them.

Isaac hailed from a well-respected, prominent trading family in Ophir. His family's name was synonymous with prosperity and integrity. Sarah saw in Isaac a partner who could help bring her dreams to fruition. They embarked on a journey together, combining their strengths and pooling their resources to build a legacy of wealth.

Sarah and Isaac's bond grew stronger with each passing day. Their shared vision of financial independence united them, and they resolved to create a thriving business empire that would benefit not only their families but also the people of Ophir.

Together, they ventured into various sectors of trade—exquisite fabrics, precious gems, spices, and rare artifacts. Sarah's excellent eye for quality and ability to forge strong relationships

with suppliers and clients proved indispensable. Isaac's astute financial acumen and strategic thinking enabled them to navigate the ever-changing market tides.

However, their journey was not without its challenges. Ophir's marketplace was fiercely competitive, with established trading families holding significant sway. Sarah and Isaac, despite their ambition and determination, faced skepticism and resistance from some quarters.

One of their most significant early setbacks occurred when a key supplier abruptly terminated their contract, leaving Sarah and Isaac in a precarious position. This sudden loss threatened to undo all their hard work and jeopardize their budding enterprise.

In the face of adversity, they turned to their shared principles of perseverance and integrity.

They combed through their network of contacts and suppliers, determined to find an alternative source. Through relentless effort and negotiations, they secured a new supplier and strengthened their relationships within the trading community.

Another challenge arose when a natural disaster disrupted their supply chain. A devastating storm had washed out crucial routes for the spices they imported, jeopardizing their inventory and causing delays that strained their financial resources.

But Sarah and Isaac refused to succumb to despair. Instead, they diversified their portfolio, investing in ventures that could sustain them during difficult times. They also improved their disaster preparedness, ensuring that their supply chain was more resilient in the face of unforeseen challenges.

As the years passed, Sarah and Isaac encountered various other obstacles—fluctuations in commodity prices, competition from larger traders, and the occasional betrayal by those they had trusted. However, their unwavering commitment to their vision and each other carried them through.

With every challenge they overcame, they grew wiser and more resilient. They adapted their strategies, diversified their investments, and, most importantly, remained true to their integrity, fairness, and community engagement principles. They also gave back to Ophir by supporting local initiatives and offering mentorship to aspiring entrepreneurs.

Their journey was far from easy but filled with lessons and victories. They learned that success wasn't just about amassing wealth; it was about the journey, the growth, and the impact they had on their community. As they continued to navigate the ever-changing landscape of Ophir's business world, Sarah and Isaac knew that they were on the cusp of something great—a flourishing business empire that would not only benefit them but also the city they loved.

As their business flourished, Sarah and Isaac remained committed to integrity, fairness, and social responsibility. They created employment opportunities for the people of Ophir, uplifting families and communities. They invested in education and skill development, recognizing that knowledge was the true key to unlocking prosperity.

Sarah and Isaac's legacy extended far beyond their financial success. They used their wealth and influence to support charitable endeavors, funding initiatives that improved the lives of the less fortunate. Their generosity knew no bounds, and they became renowned for their philanthropy and benevolence.

Years turned into decades, and Sarah and Isaac's empire continued to grow, transcending the boundaries of Ophir. They eventually married, and their children, raised with the same values of hard work, integrity, and compassion, joined them in the business, carrying the torch of their parents' legacy.

As time passed, Sarah further understood that true wealth went beyond monetary riches and lay in the legacy she and her husband would leave behind. She set out to cultivate a culture of financial literacy and empowerment among widows and young orphans.

She established a foundation dedicated to educating orphans, providing workshops for widows, teaching and training them in the art of wealth creation, and imparting knowledge and skills that would empower them to break free from the shackles of financial insecurity. She believed that when citizens prospered, the nation prospered.

Her foundation became a beacon of hope, inspiring countless women and children in Ophir and beyond to unleash their potential and embark on their journeys of financial independence. Sarah's name became associated with empowerment and courage, and her story served as a testament to the transformative power of determination and vision.

As Sarah grew older, her health began to decline. Recognizing that her time on earth was limited, she called together her loved ones and shared her insights. She urged them to continue the legacy of wealth creation and social responsibility and embrace the values that had guided their family for generations.

Sarah's legacy reverberated through the ages. The foundation she had laid catalyzed change, uplifting generations to come.

Ophir celebrated her name, and the impact of her endeavors echoed far beyond its borders.

To this day, Sarah's legacy lives on in the hearts and minds of those who dare to dream and strive for financial independence. Her story serves as a reminder that wealth is not merely a measure of possessions but a reflection of one's character and their impact on the world stage.

And so, in the golden city of Ophir, Sarah's name is synonymous with prosperity, empowerment, and the relentless

pursuit of creating a better world through the power of wealth. Her legacy continues to inspire, lighting the way for future generations to build their own legacies of abundance and impact.

> —Gold is the most potent force in the hands of man to check undue expansion of government power, as well as to prevent the irresponsible government from debasing the currency. -Richard M. Nixon

THREE

Connie's Quest For Financial Independence

Constance was a dressmaker who lived in Ophir, nestled amidst verdant hills and shimmering rivers. Her spirit was as resilient as the ancient trees that lined the streets, but her circumstances were filled with adversity. Determined to carve a path to financial freedom, she embarked on a quest to test her resilience, illuminate her strength, and reveal the true power of perseverance.

Constance was born into a modest family; her parents, having faced their share of challenges, had instilled in her key values such as hard work, integrity, and the pursuit of knowledge. As Constance grew older, she witnessed her family's struggles to make ends meet, and a burning desire to liberate herself from the constraints of financial insecurity lit within her.

One day, as she navigated the bustling markets of Ophir, Constance overheard talk about a prosperous merchant named Raphael. Stories of his astute business acumen,

compassion for the less fortunate, and unwavering commitment to justice rippled through the city. Her heart fluttered with a glimmer of hope as she absorbed these tales. She resolved to seek Raphael's wisdom, believing that his guidance could illuminate a path to financial independence.

With determination fueling her every step, she continuously searched through the cobblestone streets of Ophir, her spirit buoyed by the tales of Raphael's benevolence. After days of relentless pursuit, she arrived at Raphael's opulent estate, nestled on a hill overlooking the city. The mansion was a monument to his success and a symbol of the heights she aspired to reach.

Taking a deep breath, Constance approached the grand entrance, her heart pounding with anticipation. After ringing the bell, the doors swung open, revealing a world of luxury beyond anything she'd ever imagined. She was led into a lavish room adorned with golden tapestries, where Raphael sat, surrounded by advisors and associates.

Raphael, a man of commanding presence and warmth, excused himself at Connie's entrance and beckoned her forward. —Welcome, young lady, ‖ he said, greeting her witha smile. —What is your purpose for coming here?

Constance approached Raphael, her voice steady but filled with vulnerability. —Sir, my name is Constance, and I yearn to break free from the chains of financial insecurity. I heard of your reputation for exceeding success and generosity and have come to seek your knowledge and counsel to help me discover a way towards independence.

Raphael nodded, his eyes filled with empathy. He recognized the fire within her, the unyielding determination that burned in her gaze. —Constance, he began, his voice resonant and articulate, —Financial independence is a journey that requires patience, resourcefulness, doggedness, and a steadfast commitment to growth. I sense an earnest desire within you. Allow me to share with you the lessons I have learned along the way.

Constance was directed to a comfortable chair, where she sat, her gaze fixed on Raphael, ready to absorb every word that fell from his lips.

Constance, Raphael declared, —the first step towards financial independence is cultivating a strong work ethic. Embrace every opportunity, no matter how humble it may seem. Show dedication, integrity, and a willingness to learn. Your commitment to excellence will lay the foundation for success.‖

Connie listened attentively, taking notes and engraving his words in her mind. She was reminded yet again of the value of hard work and the importance of nurturing a reputation built on trust and reliability. She vowed to seize every opportunity that presented itself and to pour her heart into every endeavor.

Raphael continued, —The second principle is the power of financial intelligence. Educate yourself in matters of money, understand the intricacies of commerce, and seek out growth opportunities. By acquiring financial knowledge, you will empower yourself to make informed decisions and navigate the complexities of the market. Do these by investing in books and resources that will facilitate your goal.

Connie's determination intensified as she assimilated Raphael's words. She took mental note of the fact that knowledge was the key to unlocking her financial potential.

She pledged to immerse herself in finance, learn the language of commerce, and become a master of financial intelligence.

The third principle, Raphael shared, —is embracing change and adaptability. The world of business is ever- evolving, and success lies in one's ability to anticipate and adapt to shifting landscapes. Be open to innovation, embrace new technologies, and foster a spirit of adaptability. In doing so, you position yourself at the forefront of progress.

Constance nodded, her mind filled with possibilities. She understood the significance of staying ahead of the curve and embracing change rather than shying away. She resolved to remain agile, embrace innovation, and adapt to the ever-changing tides of commerce.

Raphael's voice grew softer as he imparted the fourth principle. —Constance, one must develop a strong network of relationships to attain financial independence. Surround yourself with people who inspire and support you; seek out mentors who can guide you on your journey and foster connections that expand your horizons. Together, we achieve more than we ever could alone.

Connie's heart swelled with gratitude as she realized the importance of community. The power of collaboration and the support of others could propel her towards her goals. It gave her some comfort that she wouldn't have to or didn't need to figure it out alone. She made up her mind to invest in networking and building relationships with like-minded individuals who shared her vision.

With a warm smile, Raphael revealed the fifth and final principle. —Finally, the path to financial independence is paved with empathy and compassion. As you progress, remember to uplift those around you, share your knowledge, and contribute to society's betterment. By aligning your pursuit of wealth with acts of kindness, you create a legacy that extends far beyond material possessions.‖

The embers of Connie's heart lit with a profound sense of purpose as she internalized Raphael's words. She ruminated on his words, acknowledging that financial independence is not an end but a means to make a positive impact in the lives of others. She would use her prosperity to uplift the less fortunate, create opportunities for those in need, and be a beacon of hope in a world hungry for compassion.

From that day on, Constance dedicated herself to embodying the principles Raphael had imparted. She tirelessly worked, seizing every opportunity that came her way, and her reputation as a woman of integrity and reliability grew. She immersed herself in books on finance and commerce, broadening her understanding of the intricate workings of the market. She embraced change and innovation and fearlessly navigated the shifting landscape of business. Constance cultivated relationships, forming bonds with individuals who shared her vision and learning from mentors who had trodden the path to financial independence before her. Above all, she always remembered the power of empathy and compassion, extending a helping hand to those in need and using her resources to create positive change in the world.

The sun rose over the bustling city as Connie embarked on her journey to turn her dream of starting a

successful fashion brand into a reality. She had been inspired by the sage advice of Raphael, the old merchant, and felt a newfound determination in her heart. Armed with her sketches and small savings, she rented a modest workspace in a creative neighborhood.

The initial days were filled with excitement as Connie designed her first collection. Her fingers danced over fabrics, and her sewing machine hummed with promise. Friends and family rallied around her, offering encouragement and occasional assistance. But as the weeks turned into months, Connie began encountering the first signs of adversity.

First, there were the financial struggles. Despite Raphael's advice, Connie found it challenging to stick to her budget. Unforeseen expenses, from equipment repairs to material costs, kept piling up. Her initial savings dwindled faster than she had anticipated.

Connie worked tirelessly, often late into the night, pouring her heart and soul into every piece she crafted. However, the fashion world proved to be a tough arena. Competing brands with bigger budgets and established reputations seemed to overshadow her efforts.

Her designs were unique, but getting noticed amidst the noise of the industry was a formidable task.

Raphael's words echoed in her mind: "It's not the storms that define us; it's how we weather them." Connie clung to those words like a lifeline.

She reached out to mentors and sought advice from seasoned designers, absorbing every nugget of wisdom they offered. She learned about marketing, networking, and the importance of building a brand identity.

As the months turned into a year, Connie's determination remained unshaken. However, the challenges continued to mount. She faced production delays, shipping mishaps, and even a fashion show disaster where her carefully crafted garments met an unexpected downpour on the runway.

Financially, Connie was stretched thin. She had to make difficult choices, like cutting back on marketing efforts and temporarily downsizing her workspace. She even took on a part-time job to make ends meet, a far cry from the vision of success she had envisioned after her meeting with Raphael.

But through it all, Connie's passion and resilience burned brighter than ever. She refused to let setbacks define her.

She revisited her designs, refined them further, and honed her business acumen.

Slowly but steadily, her brand, LWÄNDILĚ Çhiĉ, began to gain a small following of loyal customers who appreciated the authenticity and heart that went into each piece.

The turning point came when a local boutique owner stumbled upon Connie's creations. Impressed by the craftsmanship and unique designs, the boutique agreed to carry her collection. It was a small step, but it brought a glimmer of hope. Word-of-mouth began to spread, and soon, other boutiques expressed interest in her work.

Connie's journey was far from over, but she had learned to embrace the process, the challenges, and the growth that came with it. She had weathered the initial storm, and while she was not yet a household name in the fashion world, she was steadily making a name for herself, one stitch at a time.

As she continued to navigate the unpredictable seas of the fashion industry, Connie often thought of Raphael and the invaluable wisdom he had shared with her. She knew that success wasn't a destination but a journey, and she was determined to see it through.

And so the young designer pressed on, with dreams in her heart, a sewing needle in her hand, and the wisdom of a wise old merchant as her guiding light, ready to face whatever challenges lay ahead on her path to success.

Over the years, Connie's dogged pursuit of her passion, along with the crucial advice she received from Raphael, yielded astounding results.

Her dedication to the ideals of creativity, invention, and meticulous attention to detail

propelled her to fulfill her dreams. She built a flourishing fashion empire that spanned diverse cities and states.

Her empire thrived, expanding its reach far beyond the borders of Ophir. With each passing year, her influence grew, and her designs became coveted works of art in the fashion industry. She established flagship stores in bustling capitals around the world, in Axum, Meroe, Alexandria, and as far as Athens, each exuding the unique essence of her brand.

LWÄNDILĚ Çhiĉ, became known not only for its exquisite garments but also for its commitment to ethical practices and sustainability. Connie prioritized the responsible sourcing of materials and ensured fair treatment and fair wages for her employees, fostering a culture of empowerment and growth within her organization. She believed that true success lay not only in monetary gain but also in positively impacting the world.

The growth of Connie's fashion company created numerous employment opportunities for talented people who shared her vision.

She sought out promising designers, skilled artisans, and committed professionals to join her team. These individuals were nurtured and empowered to develop their creative potential under Connie's supervision and direction, contributing to the empires' growth and success.

Beyond her business achievements, Connie's story inspired countless aspiring entrepreneurs and individuals seeking financial freedom.

Her journey from humble beginnings to building an international fashion empire resonated with people from all walks of life. She became a symbol of possibility, showing that dreams can become reality with passion, perseverance, and a commitment to one's principles.

Constance, the resilient young woman who dared to dream of financial freedom, emerged as a shining example of the power of tenacity and the incredible potential within every individual.

Her journey not only transformed her life but also ignited a spark in the hearts of those who followed in her footsteps. The city of Ophir celebrated her accomplishments, and her legacy endured, forever etched in the annals of her history.

> —Gold is a currency, not a commodity. It's timeless, universal, and a store of value.‖ - Jim Rickards

FOUR

Josiah And The Power Of Persistence

A young engineer, Josiah, lived in the city of Ophir, known for his thriving trade and majestic architecture. His journey exemplifies the power of persistence and unwavering determination in the face of adversity.

Josiah came from a middle-class household, and his family engaged in the trade of precious gemstones. His father was the salesman, and his mother was the bookkeeper. She taught him all she knew as soon as he could talk—mathematics, as his first language, you might say.

In his teens, he would accompany his father during academic breaks. From a young age, he showed exceptional wisdom and an insatiable curiosity, eagerly soaking up the knowledge of the seasoned traders who frequented his family's shop.

Motivated by an immense desire to significantly impact the world, Josiah set out to broaden his understanding of trade and explore opportunities outside the walls of his family home. He enthusiastically roamed Ophir's busy markets,

observing the intricate dance of negotiations and transactions and acquiring every ounce of wisdom that wafted through the air.

One fateful day, news spread throughout the city that the king was grappling with a unique problem—an immense shortage of fresh water. The once-bountiful springs that had sustained the kingdom were running dry, leaving the people and their livelihoods at risk.

Josiah's ears perked up as he listened to the whispers in the marketplace. He sensed an opportunity to employ his knowledge and problem-solving skills to alleviate the king's plight. Driven by a resolute belief in his abilities, Josiah made his way to the royal palace, determined to present his unconventional solution.

Josiah outlined his plan to the minister in charge of Civil Works who was so impressed by Josiah's pitch that he arranged for Josiah to have an audience with the king outright.

Upon meeting the king, Josiah respectfully shared his vision—a comprehensive plan to tap into the aquifers that lay beneath Ophir. He proposed a system of intricate channels and reservoirs that would harness the untapped water resources, ensuring a sustainable supply for the kingdom's needs.

The king, impressed by Josiah's determination and innovative thinking, granted him the authority to implement his plan. With the kingdom's hopes resting on his shoulders, Josiah set to work, assembling a team of skilled engineers, architects, and laborers.

Days turned to weeks and weeks into months as Josiah and his team labored tirelessly, overcoming countless obstacles and challenges. They excavated the earth and meticulously crafted an intricate network of channels and reservoirs, ensuring every drop of water would be efficiently harnessed and distributed.

As the project neared completion, anticipation and skepticism hung in the air. The people of Ophir wondered whether Josiah's audacious plan would bear fruit and quench their parched lands. Finally, the day of reckoning arrived—a moment of truth for Josiah, his team, and his vision.

With bated breath, the city watched as water gushed through the newly constructed channels, flowing into the once-dry reservoirs. Fresh water springs erupted, nurturing the thirsty soil and bringing life back to the kingdom. The

people rejoiced, their gratitude pouring out like the precious resource they had regained.

News of Josiah's remarkable feat spread like wildfire, captivating the hearts and minds of the kingdom's inhabitants. The king, acknowledging Josiah's brilliance and dedication, bestowed upon him a position of great honor and authority—a trusted advisor in infrastructure and construction matters.

Under Josiah's guidance, Ophir flourished. The city became renowned for its bustling trade and ingenuity in solving complex problems. Josiah's reputation as a visionary leader and problem solver grew, drawing the attention of neighbouring regions and garnering respect from envoys far and wide.

Despite the accolades and accomplishments, Josiah remained humble.

He understood that true satisfaction lay not in titles or material rewards but in the transforming impact one could make in the lives of others. He used his position to advocate for fair trade practices, ensuring tradesmen and merchants, both large and small, had equal opportunities to thrive.

Josiah also implemented the value of education and knowledge sharing. He established schools and institutes,

inviting scholars and experts to share their insights with the next generation. Josiah believed that empowering the youth with the proper knowledge and tools would secure the kingdom's future prosperity.

As the years passed, Josiah's name became known for his persistence, innovations, and steadfast commitment to improving the lives of the people of Ophir. His story spread far and wide, inspiring those facing seemingly insurmountable challenges.

To this day, Josiah's legacy lives on. His name echoes through the corridors of trade, reminding aspiring entrepreneurs and problem solvers that with persistence and confidence in their abilities, they, too, can overcome obstacles and leave a lasting impact on the world.

As Josiah's reputation as a visionary engineer grew, so did his passion for advancing the engineering field in Ophir. He knew that the power of engineering extended far beyond solving immediate problems; it had the potential to shape the future and drive progress.

His fierce passion for imparting knowledge led Josiah to establish engineering institutes and invite engineers worldwide to share their expertise.

The institutes became hubs of innovation and collaboration, where engineers from diverse backgrounds converged to exchange ideas and push the boundaries of the seemingly impossible.

Josiah's dedication to engineering education extended to the youth of Ophir. He believed in nurturing the talents of aspiring engineers from a young age, providing scholarships and mentorship programs to cultivate their skills and ignite their passions. Through these initiatives, Josiah aimed to build a strong foundation for future generations, empowering them to carry forward his vision and continue driving the progress of Ophir.

Under Josiah's leadership, Ophir became a center for engineering excellence, attracting ambitious engineers who sought to be part of the city's remarkable growth and development. The streets buzzed excitedly as groundbreaking engineering projects took shape, from grand architectural marvels to innovative infrastructural solutions.

Josiah's engineering prowess was not limited to water management alone. He embraced the challenges presented by other aspects of Ophir's development, applying his engineering expertise to enhance transportation systems, fortify the city's defenses, and create sustainable energy solutions.

His multidisciplinary approach and ability to think holistically propelled Ophir to new heights of prosperity and excellence.

As the years passed, Josiah's commitment to engineering and the betterment of society remained strong.

He dedicated his later years to philanthropic endeavors, using his wealth to improve the lives of the less fortunate.

His impact extended beyond Ophir's borders, from building sustainable housing for the impoverished to designing innovative solutions for clean water access in underserved communities.

He is celebrated as a symbol of engineering excellence and the power of persistence. His story serves as a testament to the transformative potential of engineering, showing how anyone driven by passion and determination, can shape the destiny of a nation and leave an enduring legacy of progress.

> —Gold is the only thing that can't be printed. It's limited in supply, unlike fiat money.‖ - Robert Kiyosaki

FIVE

Esther's Debt And The Blessing Of UNkulunkulu

In the magnificent city of Ophir, where grandeur and opulence filled the air, lived a young street vendor named Esther. She possessed a vibrant spirit like the golden sunsets that bathed the city, but her heart was burdened by a heavy debt that seemed insurmountable. Determined to free herself from its shackles, she set out on a journey that tested her and led her to the true nature of fortune.

Esther's debt had accumulated over time due to unforeseen circumstances and misguided decisions. Esther had always been a diligent and hardworking vendor, selling her beautifully woven fabrics in the bustling marketplace of Ophir. Her creations were admired for their intricate designs, and she had built a loyal customer base. Life was modest but comfortable until an unforeseen circumstance sent her world into a tailspin. One fateful day, a close friend faced a dire financial crisis.

They appealed to Esther's compassion, explaining their predicament and pleading for help. Esther, guided by her kind heart, agreed to lend her friend a significant sum of money to tide them over. She believed it was a temporary solution and trusted that her friend would repay the debt as soon as they got back on their feet.

Months passed, and Esther's friend struggled to recover from their financial woes. The promised repayment never materialized. The weight of the unpaid debt began to bear down on Esther's finances. She found herself juggling bills and barely making ends meet as the interest on the loan she had taken to help her friend grew increasingly burdensome.

To compound her woes, Esther faced a sudden increase in the prices of the materials she needed for her wares. Her supplier, sensing her desperation and lack of alternative options, exploited the situation by doubling the prices. Esther had no choice but to raise her prices significantly to compensate for the increased costs. This, unfortunately, led to a decrease in her sales as her loyal customers began to look elsewhere for more affordable options. Esther was now trapped in a vicious cycle of debt.

She had taken a loan from a shady lender who charged exorbitant

interest rates and employed ruthless tactics. The loan shark's relentless pressure and threats added to her misery. Esther

had initially believed that the loan would serve as a temporary solution to her financial woes, but it had turned into a relentless burden.

As the debt grew, Esther's once-thriving business faltered. The weight of financial obligations made it difficult for her to invest in her inventory, expand her product line, or even pay for the basic needs of her household. She struggled to make the minimum payments on her mounting debts, and the interest continued to accumulate.

Esther had become ensnared in a debt trap, one that seemed impossible to escape. The once-vibrant street vendor, who had once dreamed of creating a legacy of financial stability for herself and her family, now found herself on the precipice of financial ruin.

The glittering city of Ophir, once a symbol of prosperity, now felt like a labyrinth of despair, and Esther was lost within it.

Her story, like that of many others, highlighted the dangers of predatory lending practices and the devastating impact of unexpected financial setbacks. As Esther's debts spiraled out of control, she yearned for a lifeline, a glimmer of hope that would help her navigate her way out of this grim situation.

One fateful day, while she was manning her small stall in the marketplace, a kind-hearted stranger named Gabriel stopped by. He was a retired banker, now enjoying a peaceful life in Ophir. Gabriel had a keen eye for people in distress and sensed Esther's troubles.

Approaching Esther with a warm smile, he struck up a conversation. Esther, worn down by the weight of her debt, confided in him about her predicament. Gabriel listened empathetically, recognizing that she had fallen victim to unscrupulous lending practices.

"Esther," he began, "you're in a dangerous cycle of debt. These loan sharks prey on people's desperation and trap them in a never-ending cycle. I've seen this happen far too often."

Esther looked up at Gabriel, her eyes filled with a glimmer of hope. "What can I do, Gabriel? I'm drowning in debt, and I can't see a way out."

Gabriel nodded thoughtfully. "The first step is to get out of this loan agreement. I can help you with that.

We'll approach the authorities and expose the lender's unlawful practices. But that's just the beginning. You also need to learn how to protect yourself from such schemes in the future."

Over the following weeks, Gabriel kept his promise. With his expertise and the assistance of legal authorities, they managed to extricate Esther from the clutches of the loan shark. However, Esther knew that simply escaping one debt wouldn't secure her financial future. She asked Gabriel for his counsel.

Gabriel advised Esther that she needed a mentor and offered to introduce her to an associate who could help in her business. She leaped at the opportunity and thanked Gabriel for his support.

Gabriel made the necessary arrangements with his associate, Abraham, giving her directions and a letter of introduction.

Not wanting to waste any time, the very next day, Esther made her way through Ophir, asking various people for directions to his residence. She finally arrived at the modest home of Abraham, a wise man known for understanding the elusive nature of fortune.

Upon entering the humble dwelling, Esther's eyes met Abraham's gaze, filled with wisdom and compassion. —Greetings, young lady. Gabriel has told me a lot about you‖ he said, his voice carrying the weight of experience. —How are you? —I am well thank you, she replied. —I sense your burden—you have been through a lot my dear, come sit with me, and we will unload it together.

Esther took a seat, overwhelmed by the overflowing warmth and empathy radiating from him.

—Esther,‖ Abraham began, —I shall impart upon you the secrets of fortune, for it is known, though Elohim governs the destinies of men, blessing some with abundance whilst others appear neglected. It is not so; therefore, fear not, for there are ways to navigate the intricate maze of fortune and liberate oneself from the grip of debt and poverty.‖

Esther listened intently, her curiosity ignited by the mention of UNKulunkulu and His role in shaping one's financial fate.

Fortune, or what some may call _luck ', is not a mere rollof the dice, Abraham explained. —It is the confluence of preparation and opportunity. To change your financial destiny, you must understand and apply the principles laid out in the Torah.

First, Abraham proclaimed, —prepare yourself thoroughly so you can seize opportunities when they presentthemselves. Grow in value and continuously add new skills to your repertoire. Keep a watchful eye on the currents of Ophir's economy, identify emerging trends, and be prepared to act swiftly when fortune's door opens.

Esther's mind whirred with possibilities. Until now, she had been consumed by her debt, unaware of the opportunities surrounding her. Abraham's words kindled a fire within her, igniting a determination to become more vigilant and proactive.

Second, cultivate relationships with those who possess the intelligence and means to aid you, Abraham continued.

Connect with mentors; seek counsel from those who have experienced both fortune and misfortune. Surround yourself with individuals who can offer guidance and open doors to new possibilities.

Esther nodded, bearing in mind the value of building a network of support. She had always been a solitary soul, but seeking guidance from others resonated within her. She would genuinely need the wisdom and insights that could help her navigate the complex tapestry of fortune. Abraham's voice grew softer as he continued, saying,

UNKulunkulu favors those who take calculated risks. While caution is necessary, fortune smiles upon those who step outside their comfort zones. Be willing to embrace change, explore new ventures, and adapt to shifting tides of opportunity.

Esther's pulse quickened at the thought of taking risks. She had always been cautious, fearing failure and the consequences it might bring. But now she understood that

fortune favors the bold, who are willing to step into the unknown and seize the chances for a brighter future.

Emboldened by Abraham's teachings, Esther began to apply the three principles in her life. She immersed herself in keenly observing the ebb and flow of commerce. She sought other mentors, conversing with successful merchants and learning from their experiences. Most importantly, she mustered the courage to take calculated risks, embracing opportunities that she once would have shied away from.

As time passed, Esther's efforts bore fruit. She discovered a niche within the market where her unique skills and talents could flourish. She persuaded some of the merchants coming from the East with textiles and spices to give her sole rights to the distribution of their goods.

With each calculated risk she took, her debt gradually diminished, and her financial prospects improved. Her customer base and network grew exponentially, and subsequently, demand for textiles and spices outpaced her supply.

One day, an unexpected turn of events brought Esther into contact with a wealthy merchant named Haman. He was impressed with her business acumen and offered her a partnership that would not only help her with her supply problems but also help her business grow beyond her wildest dreams.

He offered to supply her with all the spices and textiles she could sell; however, she had to agree to be his exclusive distributor. She would have to stop working with all the other merchants.

As Esther pondered this tempting proposition, a feeling of unease settled within her. She sensed that Haman's intentions were not pure, and his desire for control and dominance could have unwanted consequences. Drawing on the wisdom she acquired from Abraham, she recognized the need to tread carefully, not succumb to greed, and consider the long-term implications of her decisions.

With a heavy heart, Esther declined Haman's offer, choosing instead to forge her own path, guided by the

principles and wisdom imparted by Abraham. She realized that true liberation from debt and financial success required integrity, discernment, and the ability to resist short-term gains that could compromise long-standing partnerships and long-term stability.

As the years unfolded, Esther's journey inspired many in Ophir.

Her adherence to the principles of fortune allowed her to rise above her circumstances, transforming her debt into a stepping stone towards prosperity. She became a ray of hope, teaching others the importance of seizing opportunities,

cultivating relationships, and taking calculated risks in their pursuit of financial freedom.

As a result, the young street vendor, who had once been burdened by debt, emerged as a testament to the transformative power of fortune. Through her journey, she liberated herself and became a guiding light for countless others in the majestic city of Ophir, helping them navigate the maze of fortune and experience fulfilling lives.

SIX

Ethan's Journey To Wealth

Ethan was a scribe residing in the prosperous city of Ophir, nestled amidst lush valleys and golden plains. Despite his unwavering dedication and excellent craftsmanship, Ethan was trapped in a cycle of financial struggle. Determined to change his circumstances, he embarked on a journey to seek wisdom and unlock the secrets of wealth.

Ethan had heard whispers of a renowned sage named Solomon, whose teachings had transformed the lives of many in Ophir. Driven by an insatiable thirst for knowledge, Ethan went on a pilgrimage to find Solomon and learn from his wisdom.

The road to Solomon's abode was arduous and winding, but Ethan pressed on, fuelled by his desire for financial independence. Finally, after days of traveling through verdant forests and crossing cascading rivers, he arrived at the entrance of Solomon's humble dwelling.

With a heart filled with anticipation, Ethan knocked on the door. Moments later, it creaked open, revealing the wise sage himself, surrounded by an air of wisdom and authority.

Greetings, esteemed sage Solomon, Ethan said with reverence. —I am Ethan, a scribe burdened by the weight of financial hardship. I come seeking your guidance and wisdom so that I may find a path to prosperity.

Solomon's eyes twinkled, extending his hand in welcome.

Of course, young Ethan, welcome, he replied warmly.

Enter, and together, we shall unravel the secrets that will guide you on your journey to financial abundance.

Ethan stepped inside, his senses captivated by the scent of incense and the aura of wisdom that permeated the air. He settled into a cushioned seat, ready to absorb the wisdom that Solomon was about to impart.

Solomon began, his voice resonating with authority and gentle compassion. —Ethan, I shall reveal to you the _Seven Cures for a Lean Purse,' a principle that shall illuminate your path to financial prosperity.

Ethan leaned forward, his eyes and ears fixed on Solomon's every word, eager to absorb the wisdom about to be shared.

Handing Ethan a drink, he continued. —The first cure, Solomon began, —is to start saving a portion of earnings diligently. Set aside at least one-tenth of your income and guard it with care. This reserve shall serve as a foundation for your future wealth.

Ethan nodded, acknowledging the importance of this principle. Until now, he had squandered his earnings without thinking about the future. Solomon's words ignited a resolve within him.

Solomon continued, —The second cure is to control your expenditures. Distinguish between your needs and wants, and exercise prudence in your spending. Avoid wastefulness and the trappings of excessive luxury. By living within your means, you create room for financial growth.

Ethan's mind wandered to the times he had fallen prey to indulgences and unnecessary expenses. The notion of practicing restraint and mindful spending hit him deeply.

—The third cure is to make your gold multiply, Solomon declared. —Seek opportunities to invest your savings wisely. Let your money grow through compounding. Be astute in your choices and seek counsel from experienced individuals.

Ethan's eyes widened in realization. He had never considered the idea of his money working for him. The concept of investment sparked a new-found passion in him.

Solomon's voice grew even more captivating as he revealed the fourth cure, saying, —Guard your treasure against loss. Be cautious in your investments and business dealings. Seek advice from those with integrity and proven success. Do not let greed blind you; protect your hard-earned assets.‖

Ethan nodded solemnly, understanding the need for caution and wise decision-making. He had witnessed others fall victim to reckless ventures and deceitful schemes, and Solomon's words served as a reminder to tread carefully.

—The fifth cure is to make your dwelling a profitable investment,‖ Solomon continued. —Avoid lavishing expenses on your living arrangements. Instead, seek properties and assets that generate income. By turning your home into a source of revenue, you create a path to long-term wealth.‖

Ethan contemplated the wisdom of this cure. Until now, he had neglected the potential of his dwelling to contribute to his financial well-being.

The idea of owning income- generating properties sparked a newfound sense of possibility within him.

Solomon's voice softened as he shared the sixth cure,

—Ensure a future income. Prepare for the uncertainties that lie ahead by creating multiple streams of income. Seek diverse sources of wealth that will shield you from unexpected hardships.

Ethan nodded in agreement. Until now, he had been living in constant fear of losing his only source of income. The notion of multiple streams of wealth gave him hope for a more secure future.

Finally, Solomon imparted the seventh and last cure, saying, Increase your ability to earn. Acquire knowledge, skills, and expertise in your chosen field. Seek continual personal growth and improvement. By investing in yourself, you open doors to greater opportunities.

Ethan's eye gleamed with determination. He had always been a diligent scribe, but the idea of continuous learning and self-improvement resonated deeply within him. He understood that his success was intricately tied to his abilities and dedication.

Over the following months, Ethan diligently applied the Seven Cures for a Lean Purse to his life. He set aside a portion of his earnings, implemented mindful spending and embarked on a journey of financial education. He sought guidance from experienced investors and began exploring opportunities for wise investments.

With each passing day, Ethan's financial situation began to transform. His savings grew, and he made his first foray into the world of investment, guided by the wisdom he had received from Solomon.

He became known for his prudenceand integrity in business dealings, attracting opportunities and partnerships that further enhanced his wealth.

Ethan's journey to wealth became a testament to the power of wisdom and disciplined action as the years went by. By applying the —Seven Cures to a Lean Purse, he emerged as a pillar of financial success in the thriving city of Ophir.

His journey served as an inspiration for many others, encouraging them on their paths to prosperity.

And so, Ethan, who once experienced financial hardship, became a testament and living embodiment of the wisdom he had acquired.

His journey from struggle to abundance illuminated the way for countless others to pursue wealth and financial independence in Ophir.

> —"If you don't trust gold, do you trust the logic of taking a beautiful pine tree, worth about $4,000-$5,000, cutting it up, turning it into pulp and then paper, putting some ink on it, and then calling it one billion dollars?" – Kenneth J. Gerbino

SEVEN

Seven Practical Steps To Cure An Empty Bank Account:

Increase your reserve: Begin by saving a portion of your monthly income. For example, deposit 10% of your monthly earnings into a separate savings account. This consistent saving habit will gradually increase your bank balance over time.

- **Control your expenditures:**

Practice mindful spending and avoid frivolous expenses. For instance, create a monthly budget and track your expenses to identify areas where you can cut back. Allocate your resources more wisely by distinguishing between needs and wants.

- **Make your gold multiply:**

Seek profitable investment opportunities to increase your bank balance. Consider starting a business, investing in real estate, or farming.

It is never too early to start. If you live in an urban area, research and invest in a diversified portfolio of stocks or cryptocurrencies, aiming for long-term growth and potential dividends. No matter where you live, learning to trade forex is always an opportunity not to be missed.

- **Guard your treasures from loss:**

Protect your assets and be cautious with investments. Conduct thorough research and seek expert advice before making any financial decisions. For example, if you're considering investing in a new business venture, conduct a comprehensive risk analysis and due diligence to minimize potential losses.

- **Make of thy dwelling a profitable investment:**

Own your home or invest in real estate. Instead of spending money on rent, consider buying a property that can appreciate over time. For example, purchasing a home or apartment can provide a place to live and a potential income stream through rental payments.

- **Ensure a future income:**

Prepare for unexpected events by obtaining insurance coverage. For instance, health insurance can protect you from exorbitant medical expenses, and life insurance can provide financial security for your loved ones.

- **Increase thy ability to earn:**

Continuously invest in yourself through education and self-improvement. Acquire new skills or pursue higher education or training to enhance your earning potential. . For example, enroll in professional courses or workshops related to your chosen field to stay updated and advance your business or career.

By following these seven principles, individuals can take control of their finances, build wealth, and secure a prosperous future.

> —Gold was a gift for Christ (Msindisi). If it's good enough for Him, It's good enough for me! ‖ – Mr. T

EIGHT

David's Secret To Wealth

Khalani was a courageous young man who possessed a keen intellect. Growing up in the low-class part of Ophir, renowned for its abundant wealth and thriving trade, he had a burning desire to unlock the secrets of wealth. He yearned to rise above his circumstances and attain financial abundance.

One fateful day, as Khalani navigated the vibrant marketplace, he overheard some people talking about a wise sage named David. Stories of David's uncanny ability to predict market trends and his remarkable wealth had spread throughout the city like wildfire. Amazed by the tales of this enigmatic figure, Khalani began to seek David to acquire counsel and uncover the secrets to his prosperity.

He began to inquire about David's residence from various traders and individuals. He encountered merchants from distant lands, artisans showcasing their exquisite wares, and the fragrant aroma of spices wafting through the air.

After days of relentless pursuit, he arrived at David's dwelling, nestled in a quiet corner of Ophir.

Khalani stood before the door with bated breath, anticipation coursing through his veins. He hesitated for a moment, contemplating the magnitude of his actions. If all he heard was true, his life would change forever. Gathering his resolve, he knocked on the door, and it swung open, revealing a serene room that was lavishly furnished.

An elegantly dressed man stood at the entrance, his eyes sparkling with wisdom and insight. —Welcome, young man. What can I do for you?‖ The man greeted him warmly.

Hello, sir, my name is Khalani. I've come by in search of a great sage, David, who is said to have vast knowledge of everything about finance. I wish to learn from him.

Welcome, Khalani. Your search has come to an end. I am David. I sense great ambition within you. Come, sit with me, tell me your desire, and together we shall forge a path to its appropriation.

Khalani eagerly settled into a comfortable chair, his gaze fixed on David. He exuded an aura of sophistication but still seemed so approachable.

David," Khalani began, his voice filled with anticipation,

I yearn to understand the path to true wealth and prosperity. Please, enlighten me with your wisdom.

David smiled, perceiving the hunger for knowledge in Khalani's eyes. —Khalani, the secret to wealth lies not in amassing vast sums of gold but in the cultivation of a wealthy mindset and mastery of certain principles. Allow me to share with you the teachings that have guided me on my journey.

Khalani leaned forward; his mind primed to receive the wisdom he was certain would transform his life.

The first principle," David declared, —is the power of vision. Have a clear vision of the future you desire. Don't envision yourself just as a prosperous individual but as a creator of value and abundance for others. Your wealth will be directly proportional to the value you bring to the market. The more people you serve, the wealthier you will be. Let your vision inspire you to take action and positively impact in the world."

Khalani listened with rapt attention. He saw the importance of aligning his thoughts and actions with his desired outcomes.

He understood that his vision would serve as a compass, guiding him through the intricate pathways of wealth. David continued, The second principle is the art of calculated risk-taking. Wealth is not achieved by remaining

stagnant or playing it safe. Embrace calculated risks, for they hold the potential for great rewards. Assess the potential outcomes, consider the probabilities, and take bold steps forward, knowing fortune favors the brave. Whoever is daring always wins. Never fear failure; it is a lesson in and of itself. Learn from it and move forward.

Khalani nodded, contemplating the times he had been too scared to seize opportunities. David's words ignited a fire within him, an intent to shed his fear and embrace the transformative power of risk.

The third principle is the mastery of financial intelligence, David shared. —Acquire the knowledge, skills, and understanding of financial concepts and principles that enable you to make informed and effective decisions regarding personal and business finances. This encompasses a range of abilities, including financial literacy, analysis, planning, and management.

David explained further. —Having financial intelligence means comprehending and navigating various aspects of

finance, such as budgeting, investing, saving, debt management, risk assessment, and understanding financial markets. It involves understanding key financial terms, reading and interpreting financial statements, and being aware of the impact of economic factors on financial decisions.

Financial intelligence also involves making sound investment choices and strategies to achieve financial goals. It requires staying informed about market trends, economic indicators, and changes in financial regulations. Furthermore, financial intelligence includes adapting to changing circumstances and adjusting financial plans and investments accordingly.

Developing financial intelligence is important for you personally and your business, as it empowers you to make informed decisions that can lead to financial stability, growth, and wealth accumulation. It provides a foundation for managing finances effectively, planning for the future, and achieving long-term financial security.

Khalani marveled at the depth of David's teachings. He realized that to truly amass wealth, he needed to expand his financial literacy and cultivate a deep understanding of the economic landscape.

David went on. —The secret to wealth lies in the cultivation of positive habits. Exercise discipline and cultivate habits that support your financial goals. Save diligently, live within your means, and invest wisely. With these habits, you create a strong foundation upon which wealth can flourish.

Remember, cultivating positive habits is a journey that requires patience, consistency, and self-compassion. Focusing on small, gradual changes and staying committed to your goals can gradually transform your behaviors and enhance various areas of your life.

Khalani marveled at the significance of habits shaping one's financial destiny—that small, consistent actions could pave the way to long-term prosperity.

With a glint, David revealed the fifth and final principle.

Khalani, the ultimate secret to wealth is the power of generosity.

Cultivate a spirit of giving, for true wealth is not measured solely by what one possesses but by what one gives. Share your blessings, uplift others, and contribute to the betterment of society. You create abundance and a positive ripple effect by sowing seeds of kindness and generosity.

Khalani's heart swelled with compassion as he internalized David's words. He realized that wealth extended far beyond material possessions, encompassing the richness of human connection and the ability to make a difference in the lives of others.

From that day forward, Khalani dedicated himself to embodying David's principles. He immersed himself in books on finance, sought mentors who had achieved financial success, and took calculated risks that expanded his horizons. He developed a disciplined approach to saving and investing, recognizing his power to uplift himself and others.

Khalani became highly successful as time went by. He built a successful business in telecommunications that not only brought him wealth but also created employment opportunities for others. He took calculated risks that led to strategic investments, taking his company into international markets as his financial intelligence grew sharper with each passing day.

However, Khalani's true wealth resided in his positive impact on those around him, the lives he touched with his generosity, and the opportunities he created for others.

The news of Khalani's prosperity and wisdom spread throughout the city of Ophir. People from all walks of life sought his counsel, eager to learn from the once-young man who unlocked the secrets of wealth. Khalani graciously shared his knowledge, mentoring aspiring entrepreneurs and instilling the principles that had shaped his own success within them.

And so, Khalani, the ambitious young man who had embarked on a quest for wealth, emerged as a beacon of inspiration in the city of Ophir. His journey, guided by the wisdom of David and the mastery of wealth principles, became a testament to the powerful effect of a wealth mindset and the secrets that lay within every individual's grasp. His story resonated with countless others, guiding them towards a future of prosperity, fulfillment, and the true essence of wealth.

> —"Because gold is honest money it is disliked by dishonest men".‖-Ron Paul

NINE

Cultivating Good Habits

Start with self-awareness: Take the time to reflect on your current habits and identify areas where changes need to be made. Understand the objectives behind your desire to cultivate new habits and envision the benefits they will bring.

- **Set clear goals:**

Define specific and realistic goals related to the habits you want to develop. Clearly articulate what you want to achieve and why it matters to you. Break down your goals into smaller, actionable steps to make them more attainable.

- **Start small and build momentum:**

Focus on one habit at a time rather than overwhelming yourself with multiple changes. Choose a habit that aligns with your goals, and start with a manageable level of commitment. As you build consistency and confidence, gradually introduce additional positive habits.

- **Create a routine:**

Consistency is crucial when it comes to habit formation. Make it a priority to have a regular schedule or routine that incorporates your desired habits. Consistency helps reinforce behaviors and makes them more automatic over time.

- **Practice positive reinforcement:**

Reward yourself for successfully exercising your desired habits. This can be as simple as acknowledging your progress, treating yourself to something you enjoy, or finding other ways to celebrate your achievements. Positive reinforcement enhances motivation and reinforces the habit loop.

- **Monitor and track your progress:**

Keep track of your habit-related activities and progress. This can be done through journaling, using habit-tracking apps, or creating visual representations of your progress. Monitoring allows you to identify patterns, stay accountable, and adjust as needed.

- **Surround yourself with support:**

Seek support from friends, family, or like-minded individuals who can encourage and motivate you in your habit-cultivation journey.

Share your goals and progress with them, and consider finding an accountability partner or joining a supportive community.

- **Overcome obstacles and learn from setbacks:**

Recognize that setbacks and challenges are a natural part of habit-building.

When faced with obstacles, analyze what went wrong, learn from the experience, and adjust your approach if necessary.

Embrace a growth mindset that views setbacks as opportunities for learning and improvement..

- **Stay motivated and practice self-care:**

Maintain motivation by regularly reminding yourself of the benefits of your positive habits.

Take care of your physical and mental well-being through proper sleep, nutrition, exercise, and stress management.

A healthy lifestyle supports the cultivation of positive habits.

> —Gold is a currency. It is still, by all evidence, a premier currency, where no fiat currency, including the dollar, can match it.‖ - Alan Greenspan

TEN

Joseph and the Five Laws of Gold

A skilled trader named Joseph, lived in the wealthy city of Ophir, nestled amidst rolling hills and sparkling rivers. With a shrewd eye for business and unyielding determination, Joseph yearned to amass great wealth. However, his efforts seemed to yield only modest returns, leaving him dissatisfied and longing for a breakthrough.

One day, as Joseph navigated the vibrant marketplace of Ophir, he heard murmurs about a legendary merchant named Job. Whispers of Job's vast riches and extraordinary success reached Joseph's ears, piquing his curiosity. Driven by an insatiable desire for prosperity, Joseph set out to seek Job's guidance and unlock the secrets of financial abundance.

Through bustling streets and sprawling landscapes, Joseph embarked on a journey that would shape his destiny. After days of arduous travel, he arrived at the entrance of Job's grand estate, its gates gleaming with an air of prosperity.

Summoning all his courage, Joseph approached the entrance and announced his desire to meet Job. The guards,

recognizing Joseph's earnestness, led him through the grounds, into the mansion, through lavish corridors adorned with golden tapestries, and into a grand chamber where Job awaited.

Job, a distinguished figure with a commanding presence, welcomed Joseph with a warm smile. Greetings, Joseph, he said, his voice laced with wisdom. I sense your burning ambition and hunger for wealth in your eyes. Sit with me, and together, we shall uncover the secrets of financial success.

Joseph settled into a comfortable chair, his heart racing with anticipation. He had finally reached the presence of the renowned Job, and the prospect of learning from his wisdom filled him with hope.

Joseph, Job began, his voice steady and captivating, —I will impart to you the _Five Laws of Gold.' These principles will illuminate your path to wealth and unlock the secrets of financial prosperity.

Joseph leaned forward, his gaze fixed on Job, eager to absorb every word.

The first law, Job proclaimed, is to save at least one-tenth of all you earn. Cultivate the habit of setting aside a portion of your profits and guard it diligently. This reserve shall serve as a foundation for your future wealth.

Joseph's eyes widened with understanding. Until now, he had squandered his earnings on indulgences, neglecting the importance of saving. Job's words awakened a new-found sense of responsibility within him.

Job continued, —The second law is to control your expenditures. Learn to distinguish between your needs and your wants. Exercise prudence in your spending, avoiding extravagance and unnecessary luxuries. By living within your means, you create room for financial growth.‖

Joseph nodded, reflecting on his impulsive spending habits. He realized that curbing his expenses and adopting a more disciplined approach would improve his financial stability.

The third law is to make your money work for you.‖ Job declared. Seek opportunities to invest your money wisely. Let your wealth grow with the power of compound interest. Be diligent in your research and entrust your resources to ventures that promise favorable returns.‖

Joseph's mind was sparked with intrigue. He had always seen money as a means of exchange, but the concept of making it multiply was a revelation. The idea of investing strategically to generate wealth ignited a flame of curiosity within him.

Job's voice resonated with assurance as he shared the fourth law: —Guard your investments with care. Be discerning in your business dealings, seeking advice from those with proven integrity and expertise. Protect your assets from ill-conceived ventures and dubious schemes.‖

Joseph nodded solemnly, recognizing the need for caution in the pursuit of wealth. He had seen others fall victim to deceitful schemes, and Job's words served as a reminder to be vigilant and discerning.

Finally, Job unveiled the fifth and final law, —Increase your ability to earn. Acquire knowledge, skills, and expertise in your chosen field. Continuously seek ways to enhance your value and expand your earning potential. By investing in yourself, you open doors to greater opportunities.‖

Joseph's eyes shimmered with determination. He had always been diligent in his trade, but the idea of personal growth and skill development resonated deeply within him.

He understood that his success hinged on his abilities and dedication.

Over the following months, Joseph immersed himself in the teachings of the Five Laws of Gold. He diligently saved a portion of his earnings, exercised restraint in his expenditures, and embarked on a journey of self-improvement. He sought counsel from seasoned traders, expanded his knowledge of market trends, and honed his trading skills.

With each passing day, Joseph witnessed a transformation in his financial circumstances. His savings grew, and he became adept at identifying profitable investment opportunities. He forged connections with trustworthy business partners and safeguarded his resources against pitfalls.

As the years went by, Joseph's name became synonymous with financial success in the thriving city of Ophir. His journey, guided by the wisdom of Job and the Five Laws of Gold, became a beacon of hope for countless others striving for prosperity. He shared his knowledge, mentoring aspiring traders and instilling the principles that had shaped his success.

And so, Joseph, who had once yearned for wealth and struggled to find a way, emerged as a shining example of the power of wisdom and disciplined action. His journey from humble beginnings to financial abundance inspired a generation of entrepreneurs in the prosperous city of Ophir, guiding them towards a future of prosperity and realizing their dreams of financial independence.

> "The Golden rule: He who has the gold makes the rules,"
> ‖ - Anonymous

ELEVEN

The Five Laws Of Gold And Practical Applications

Gold comes gladly and in increasing quantity to any person who will put no less than one-tenth of their earnings towards creating a reserve for their future and that of their family.

This law emphasizes the importance of saving to secure a prosperous future.

1. **PRACTICAL APPLICATION:** Start by creating a budget, aiming to save at least 10% of your monthly earnings. Set up automated transfers to a separate savings or investment account to ensure consistent savings. As your income increases, consider gradually raising the percentage you save to accelerate your wealth accumulation. When opening an account, explore banks that back their reserves with gold or silver, like https://kinesis.money.

Gold labors diligently for the wise owner who finds profitable employment for it, multiplying even as flocks in a field.

This law emphasizes the importance of investing wisely to grow your wealth, encouraging the pursuit of profitable opportunities and leveraging money to generate additional income.

2. **PRACTICAL APPLICATION:** Educate yourself on various investment options, such as real estate, mutual funds, bonds, or stocks. Alternatively, consider starting a business. Conduct thorough research and seek professional advice to identify investment opportunities aligning with your financial goals and risk tolerance. Regularly review and adjust your investment portfolio to optimize returns and diversify holdings.

Gold clings to the protection of the cautious owner who invests it under the advice of those wise in handling it.

This law emphasizes the importance of risk management and seeking expert advice when making financial decisions, emphasizing the need to protect your wealth and avoid losses.

3. **PRACTICAL APPLICATION:** Collaborate with financial advisors and mentors with a proven track record and expertise in wealth management. Consult them before making major investment decisions or navigating complex financial matters. They can assist in building a well-diversified portfolio tailored to your financial situation and goals.

Gold slips away from the person who invests it in businesses or purposes with which he is unfamiliar or not approved by experts.

This emphasizes caution against blindly investing in unfamiliar ventures or following speculative trends. It stresses the importance of investing in areas you understand and seeking expert advice in the respective fields.

4. **PRACTICAL APPLICATIONS:** Conduct thorough due diligence and research before investing in any business or opportunity. Focus on industries or sectors where you have knowledge or experience. Consider investing in companies with strong fundamentals and a track record of success. Additionally, diversify your investments across different sectors to mitigate risk.

Gold flees from the person who would force it to produce impossible earnings, who follows the alluring advice of tricksters and schemers, or who trusts their own inexperience and romantic desires in investments.

This law warns against unrealistic expectations, online get-rich-quick schemes, and falling for scammers. It emphasizes the importance of making informed decisions based on sound financial principles rather than succumbing to impulsive or emotionally driven investments.

5. **PRACTICAL APPLICATION:** Be extremely cautious of investment opportunities that promise excessively high returns with little risk or require substantial upfront fees. Beware of fraud, and thoroughly research any investment or business opportunity before committing funds. Focus on long-term strategies and avoid impulsive decisions based on short-term market fluctuations or emotions.

By adhering to these Five Laws of Gold, individuals can cultivate a solid financial foundation, make wise investment decisions, and protect their wealth over time.

Remember, building wealth is a journey that requires patience, discipline, and a commitment to financial education.

> —Gold is the only money that has never failed in the 5,000-year history of its use by humans.‖ - Charles de Gaulle

TWELVE

Gold

Gold holds significant importance in biblical history and secular society, symbolizing wealth, beauty, and value. Here are some key moments related to Gold in biblical history:

In the book of Genesis, chapter 2, we are told UNkulunkulu planted a garden eastward in Eden.

GENESIS 2:10

"Now a river went out of Eden to water the garden, and from there it parted and became four riverheads. The name of the first is Pishon; it is the one that skirts the whole land of Havilah, where there is gold. And the gold of that land is good."

This was the eighth time He described something as good that He had created.

Genesis 13:2 tells us:

GENESIS 13:2

"And Abram was very rich in cattle, in silver, and in gold."

Abraham is later described as the _friend of SoNini NaNini.

UNkulunkulu commanded the Israelites to build a portable sanctuary known as the Tabernacle and later a permanent Temple. Both structures were embellished with gold, including the Ark of the Covenant, lampstands, and the Temple's walls and furnishings. The Temple itself and the interiors were gleaming with gold; it was built by Solomon, who utilized a considerable amount of gold for diverse purposes in the Temple's construction and decoration.

In a less favorable context, the book of Exodus narrates the Israelites 'ill-fated worship of a golden calf while Moses received the Ten Commandments from SoNini NaNini. This incident serves as a symbol of the perils of idolatry and the misguided veneration of material objects.

The scriptures make reference to a region called Ophir, a place associated with gold and precious materials. Ophir is cited as the source of gold for King Solomon, who engaged in frequent trade with the merchants of Ophir, dispatching fleets of ships that returned laden with precious goods.

The book of Matthew recounts the arrival of envoys (wisemen) from the East, bearing gifts for the infant Msindisi (Salvation).

Matthew 2:11 KJV

"And when they were come into the house, they saw the young child with Mary his mother, and fell down, and worshipped him: and when they had opened their treasures, they presented unto him gifts; gold, and frankincense, and myrrh"

When the Queen of Sheba visited King Solomon, the gold she presented amounted to hundreds of millions in today's monetary terms. One can only speculate about the sum presented to Msindisi. The gift represents the respect due to the individual.

These are merely glimpses into the biblical history of gold. Gold's significance in the Bible extends beyond these instances, with its mention in various other contexts, such as descriptions of heavenly imagery and metaphors for spiritual refinement.

Gold is valued highly in secular society for several reasons:

- **Rarity:**

Gold, comparatively scarce among metals, is coveted for its limited availability, enhancing its desirability and value.

- **Historical Significance:**

Valued and treasured for millennia, gold has served as a medium of exchange, a store of value, and a symbol of wealth and prestige across diverse civilizations and cultures.

- **Durability and Longevity:**

Highly resistant to corrosion, rust, and tarnish, gold exhibits exceptional longevity, remaining impervious to decay over time.

- **Universally Recognized:**

Globally acknowledged as a form of payment and wealth storage, gold's universal appeal and recognition significantly contribute to its intrinsic value.

- **Industrial and Technological Applications:**

Gold has numerous practical uses in various industries, including electronics, aerospace, medicine, and jewelry. Its unique physical and chemical properties make it valuable for these applications.

- **Economic and Political Uncertainty Hedge:**

Considered a safe-haven investment during periods of economic instability, inflation, or geopolitical uncertainty, gold serves as a means for investors to safeguard their wealth and diversify portfolios.

- **Jewelry and Ornamental Value:**

Appreciated for its aesthetic allure, gold is extensively employed in crafting jewelry and decorative items. Its beauty, rarity, and historical association with wealth and prestige contribute to its substantial value in the luxury goods market.

- **Limited Supply and Mining Costs:**

Extraction and production of gold involve considerable expense and labor, with new discoveries becoming increasingly rare, further enhancing its value.

- **Store of Value:**

Gold, maintaining its purchasing power over an extensive period, has proven its stability, acting as a reliable store of value throughout history.

It's crucial to note that the value of gold is subject to fluctuations influenced by market forces, investor sentiment, and economic conditions. While gold occupies a significant place in the global financial system and retains its allure over time, its value remains susceptible to by various factors.

> —Gold is the universal currency because it is the only one trusted by all nations.‖ - John McAfee

THIRTEEN

Why Is Gold Important?

Throughout the course of history, in the realm of commerce and trade, there has perpetually existed a method of exchanging for goods and services. The barter system represents a mode of trade where goods and services are directly swapped without the involvement of a universally accepted medium, such as currency. In a barter system, individuals or businesses engage in the direct exchange of goods or services based on their mutual needs and preferences.

Here are some key characteristics of a barter system:

Goods for Goods: Participants directly exchange goods or services in the barter system. For instance, a farmer might trade bags of wheat for a cow from a rancher, or a carpenter might offer furniture in exchange for legal services.

Lack of Currency: Unlike a monetary system, the barter system does not entail the use of a specific currency. Participants rely on the intrinsic value of the exchanged goods or services.

Double Coincidence of Wants: Bartering necessitates a double coincidence of wants, signifying that both parties involved in the trade must possess something the other desires. Finding a mutually beneficial trade can be more challenging compared to using a standardized currency.

Limited Indivisibility: Bartering becomes more complex when goods or services are not easily divisible or when the value of the traded items does not align. For instance, trading a car for a loaf of bread might be challenging due to the significant difference in value.

Barter Exchanges: Organized barter exchanges or networks, in certain cases, facilitate barter transactions by connecting individuals or businesses with complementary goods or services. These exchanges mitigate the limitations of direct bartering by providing a platform for participants to trade within the network.

It's imperative to acknowledge that while barter systems were prevalent in early human societies and still persist in specific situations today, most economies have transitioned to monetary systems founded on fiat currency. This transition aims to facilitate trade more efficiently and overcome the challenges associated with bartering.

Modern exchange systems employ Fiat Currencies as a means of exchange. Fiat Currencies, which are essentially paper money, are gradually undergoing a transformation into a digital format, eliminating physical notes and replacing them with Central Bank Digital Currencies (CBDCs). These currencies are issued and regulated by governments but lack backing by a physical commodity like gold or silver. Instead, their value is derived from the trust and confidence placed in the supporting government and legal system.

Here are some key characteristics of Fiat Currencies:

Legal Tender: Fiat Currencies are typically designated as legal tender, meaning they must be accepted as a form of payment within the country by law.

Government Control: The government or a central bank retains control over the issuance, regulation, and management of fiat currencies. They have the authority to determine the money supply, set interest rates, and implement monetary policies.

Value by Decree: The value of Fiat Currencies is established by government decree or law, not directly linked to any underlying physical commodity like gold or silver. The government declares the currency as legal tender, mandating its acceptance for transactions.

Trust and Confidence: The acceptance and use of Fiat Currencies hinge on the public's trust and confidence in the stability and integrity of the government, as well as the perceived value that can be exchanged for goods and services.

Exchangeability: Fiat Currencies are typically exchangeable for other currencies on the foreign exchange market, with exchange rates fluctuating based on various factors such as economic conditions, interest rates, and investor sentiments.

Countries adopted Fiat Currencies at different historical junctures, gradually transitioning from other forms of money (such as barter). The concept of fiat money, where currency derives its value from government declaration rather than being backed by a physical commodity like gold or silver, has evolved throughout history. Here are a few key milestones:

CHINA: The use of Fiat Currency can be traced back to ancient China during the Tang Dynasty (618–907 AD). The government issued paper money called —Jiaozi‖ as a means of exchange.

SONG DYNASTY: The use of paper money expanded during the Song Dynasty (960–1279 AD) when the government issued a standard currency known as —Guanzi.‖

SWEDEN: In the early 17th century, Sweden issued the first European banknotes as a response to the scarcity of copper and silver coins. These banknotes, known as —Stockholms Banco,‖ were backed by copper plates.

BRITISH POUND: The Bank of England was established in 1694 and began issuing paper banknotes as legal tender. These banknotes were initially backed by silver and later by gold. However, the British Pound fully transitioned to a Fiat Currency in 1931, when the gold standard was abandoned.

UNITED STATES: The United States has used various forms of money throughout its history. The Continental Congress issued paper money known as ―Continentals‖ during the American Revolutionary War but suffered from hyperinflation. In 1862, during the Civil War, the U.S. government began issuing Fiat Currency, known as ―Greenbacks.‖ The U.S. Dollar that we know today transitioned fully to a Fiat Currency in 1971, when President Richard Nixon ended the convertibility of the dollar into gold.

Global Adoption: By the mid-20th century, most countries had embraced Fiat Currencies, and today, nearly all countries use fiat money as their official means of exchange.

The global adoption of Fiat Currencies exhibited variation from country to country, with the examples above providing a general overview of the historical progress towards Fiat Currencies.

> —Paper money eventually returns to its intrinsic value—
> zero. – Voltaire

FOURTEEN

Why Is Financial Education So Important?

In scripture, we are told:

> *Genesis 13:2*
>
> "And Abram was very rich in cattle, in silver, and in gold".
>
> *2 Chronicles 20:7*
>
> "Are you not our UNKulunKulu, who drove out the inhabitants of this land before Your Bantu, and gave it to the descendants of Abraham Your friend."
>
> *James 2:23*
>
> "And the scripture was fulfillled which says, "Abraham believed UNKulunkulu and it was accounted to him for righteousness." And he was called the Friend of SoNini NaNini.

In Luke 10:25–37, we learn the parable of the Samaritan. A stranger helping a stranger in need. There are many lessons to be learned from this story. One is to help those around who are in need, and to achieve this, one must have the means to do so. As children of UNKulunkulu, we are told to love and serve; to do that, we need to have surplus resources, not just enough for ourselves. Our ancestor, Abraham, —the Friend of SoNini NaNini, and the Samaritan were persons of means. They had deep pockets that overflowed above and beyond their needs. This requires financial education.

Some benefits of financial education include:

- **Early Proficiency:**

Introducing financial literacy concepts to individuals between the ages of 12 to 18 establishes a robust foundation for effective money management.

This book seeks to thoroughly prepare readers for the financial responsibilities they will encounter as young adults.

- **Empowerment:**

Financial literacy empowers you to make informed decisions regarding your finances. Understanding concepts such as budgeting, saving, investing, and comprehending financial institutions equips you with essential skills to navigate your financial futures successfully.

- **Life Skills:**

Financial literacy, often overlooked in traditional education, is a critical life skill. The book introduces practical concepts like budgeting, debt management, credit understanding, and entrepreneurship, providing you with skills that will prove beneficial throughout your life.

- **Avoiding Common Pitfalls:**

A lack of financial education often leads many young adults into financial pitfalls, such as accumulating excessive debt or developing poor money management habits. This book serves as a guide to help readers steer clear of these common traps.

- **Building a Solid Foundation:**

The teenage years present an opportune moment to instill healthy financial habits and mindsets. By introducing financial literacy concepts early in life, the book aims to assist young readers in cultivating responsible attitudes towards money, establishing a trajectory towards long-term financial stability.

- **Parental involvement:**

We hope this introduction to financial literacy can serve as a resource for parents or guardians who may not have extensive knowledge. This can be an additional tool to educate children about money matters and start important conversations in the home about financial responsibility and wealth creation.

> —Gold is a treasure, and he who possesses it does all he wishes to in this world.‖ - Christopher Columbus

FIFTEEN

Conclusion and Author's Advice

Get educated, whether in Engineering, Medicine, Economics, or Law. Regardless of your chosen field, integrate sales and marketing into your skill set.

Start a business. Do not be afraid to fail. Learn from your mistakes. Never make the same mistake twice. Start again until you get it right.

Never give up. Nothing worth having comes easy. Anything that comes easy is probably not worth having. Finally, be of service and help as many people as you can.

In Genesis 1:28, we are told of our Maker's original plan for us:

"...Be fruitful, and multiply, and replenish the earth, and subdue it: and have dominion..."

So, we see that the scriptures are about a Heavenly King, a Creator who desires to have His children here on earth have dominion and rule over His creation. The path He set before us is smooth, but we constantly throw rocks in the way (doubt, fear, anxiety, etc.). So Msindisi came to gift us salvation and bring us back into the purpose of UNKulunkulu for us. We are taught, therefore, to pray, —Thy kingdom come...‖ In the end, His kingdom will come, and we are called to partake as kings and priests. Now, will you answer the call?

Proverbs. 16:3

"Commit thy works unto SoNini NaNini, and thy thoughts shall be established"

RECOMMENDED ACTION AND BOOKS TO STUDY

In the eight short tales we read at the beginning of this book, we learned the importance of Mentors. Guidance from those who have succeeded before us. While mentors play a crucial role, one should never underestimate the empowering force of self-reliance, achieved through deliberate self-education or, at times, re-education, coupled with focused training.

For those eager to embark on this transformative journey, we recommend several books that can serve as a catalyst. Among them, the works of Mr. Myron Golden stand out, aligning seamlessly with the core purpose of this book and its intended audience. Here are some links to his platforms, which the author has personally found not just useful but life-changing. Full disclosure: the author is an affiliate.

https://www.youtube.com/@MyronGolden/featured

https://www.makemoreofferschallenge.com/mmoc?affiliate_id=4182710

Action: Making your first Million

Upon completing this book, it's important to take action immediately. Procrastination is the killer of progress. For the following strategy, the Author expresses gratitude to Daniel Mangena and the Beyond Intention team and their Micro2Millions program link provided: https://www.c.abundanceuniversity.com/ Again, full disclosure: the author is an affiliate.

This is the concept, starting with 1 unit in your local currency (for uniformity, we will use Gold in units of Grams). Whatever the value of 1g of Gold is today in your local currency, that is your starting amount. No less, no more. How you obtain the amount will vary; the amount can be earned, saved, or gifted but not borrowed. The idea is to double the amount in increments of 1, 2, 4, 8, 16, 32, etc. Your local currency will determine the number of increments to your first million. We have provided a tracking sheet below for you to keep a record of your progress. More tools are available at Beyond Intention University if you wish to accelerate your progress.

Now, it's important that you do not cut corners at any stage. You will find some increments easier than others to achieve; you may even fail and lose what you have made

(should this happen, start again from the beginning). It is part of the learning process. Keep a journal of the action(s) you take at each stage. The second round will be far easier.

Finally, enjoy the process. There is no time limit to achieving any stage; make it something you just do as a hobby in your spare time, and in time, it will become a habit, a part of you, effortless, and second nature.

BOOKS TO STUDY:

- Genesis by Moses
- Exodus by Moses
- Deuteronomy by Moses
- Psalms by King David
- Proverbs by King Solomon
- Wisdom of Solomon by King Solomon
- Ecclesiastes by King Solomon
- The Revelation of Msindisi by John
- Rich Dad Poor Dad by Robert Kiyosaki
- As a Man Thinketh by James Allen
- The Power of Positive Thinking by Norman Vincent Peale
- Secrets of the Millionaire Mind by T. Harv Eker

- From the Trash Man to the Cash Man by Myron Golden
- Think and Grow Rich by Napoleon Hill
- Boss Moves by Myron Golden
- Why Should White Guys Have All the Fun? by Reginald F. Lewis
- Power by Robert Greene
- Becoming Supernatural by Dr. Joe Dispenza
- Wealth of Nations by Adam Smith

PLEASE NOTE THAT THIS LIST IS NOT EXHAUSTIVE, IT IS RECOMMENDED. YOU CAN FIND AS MANY SOURCES FOR KNOWLEDGE IN THIS FIELD AS YOU CAN FIND. NEVER STOP LEARNING.

ZERO TO A MILLION TRACK SHEET

STAGE	ACTION(S) TAKEN	BANK BALANCE in Gold Grams
1		1g
2		2g
3		4g
4		8g
5		16g
6		32g
7		64g
8		128g
9		256g
10		512g
11		1024g
12		2048g

13	4096g
14	8192g
15	16384g
16	32768g
17	65536g
18	131072g
19	262144g
20	524288g

N.B. At time of publication 2024 anyone with 16384 grams in Gold @ Stage 15 has earned their first Million.

Prntable PDF can be found here:

https://drive.google.com/file/d/1Gcmlug19Ueoh5B1ZxSiTiPSZFTWj7_cg/view?usp=sharing

BIBLICAL RECORDS OF THE LAND OF OPHIR

Genesis 10:29 (NLT): —Ophir, Havilah, and Jobab. All these were the sons of Joktan.

1 Kings 9:28 (NIV): —They sailed to Ophir and brought back 420 talents of gold, which they delivered to King Solomon.

1 Kings 10:11(KJV): —The navy of Hiram, that brought gold from Ophir, brought in from Ophir great plenty of almug trees, and precious stones.

1 Kings 22:48 (AMPC): —Jehoshaphat made ships of Tarshish to go to Ophir for gold, but they did not go, for the ships were wrecked at Ezion-geber.

2 Chronicles 8:108 (AMPC): —And Huram sent to him by the hand of his servants' ships and servants familiar with the sea; and they went with the servants of Solomon to Ophir together and took from there 450 talents of gold and brought them to King Solomon.

2 Chronicles 9:10 (KJV): —And the servants of Hiram and the servants of Solomon, who brought gold from Ophir, brought algum trees and precious stones.

Job 22:24 (ESV): ―If you lay gold in the dust, and gold of Ophir among the stones of the torrent-bed.‖

Job 28:16 (ESV): ―It cannot be valued in the gold of Ophir, in precious onyx or sapphire.‖

These are all the verses in the Bible that mention Ophir. They provide references to Ophir's association with gold, trade, and the ships that sailed to and from Ophir in ancient times.

In conclusion—A good man leaves an inheritance to his children's children, but the sinner's wealth is laid up for the righteous.‖(Proverbs 13:22 ESV)

Deuteronomy 6:1-2

"Now these are the commandments, the statutes, and the judgements which SoNini NaNini commanded to teach you, that ye might do them in the land whither ye go to possess it: That thou mightest fear SoNini NaNini, to keep all his statutes and his commandments, which I command thee, thou, and thy son, and thy son's son, all the days of thy life: and that thy days may be prolonged."

Joshua 1:6-8

"Be strong and of good courage: for unto this people shall you divide the land for an inheritance...Only be strong and very courageous, that you may guard to do according to all the Torah, which Moses my servant commanded you: turn not from it to the right hand or to the left, that you may prosper whithersoever you go....meditate therein day and night, that you guard to do according to all that is written therein: for then you shall make your way prosperous, and then you shall have good success.

"It is the glory of UNKulunkulu to conceal a thing: but the honour of kings to search out a matter. Prov. 25 : 2 KJV

SECULAR RECORDS OF THE LAND OF OPHIR

QUOTE FROM: THE ANCIENT RUINS OF RHODESIA WRIITEN IN 1902.
R.N. HALL AND W.G. NEAL

SUGGESTED SOUTH-EAST AFRICAN OPHIR.

All the imports brought by Hiram for King Solomon could only have been obtained in one country. His voyages were made every three years (readers should note that before colonization, Africa was viewed as one country, not 54+ separate territories). Only Africa could have furnished them altogether.

HIRAM'S "GOLD."

1. Gold was, according to biblical and secular writings, the principal export of Ophir.

2. Africa has always been known in ancient history (even today) as being the gold-producing country (continent) of the world.

3. Numerous authorities, such as Bruce, Huet, Quartremere, and Guillian, as well as the great majority of later writers on Rhodesian (Zimbabwean) ruins, in considering the historic gold output of this country (Continent), favour the claims of Monomotapa (Rhodesia, Zimbabwe) to be the OPHIR of scripture.

James Rennel 1799 map

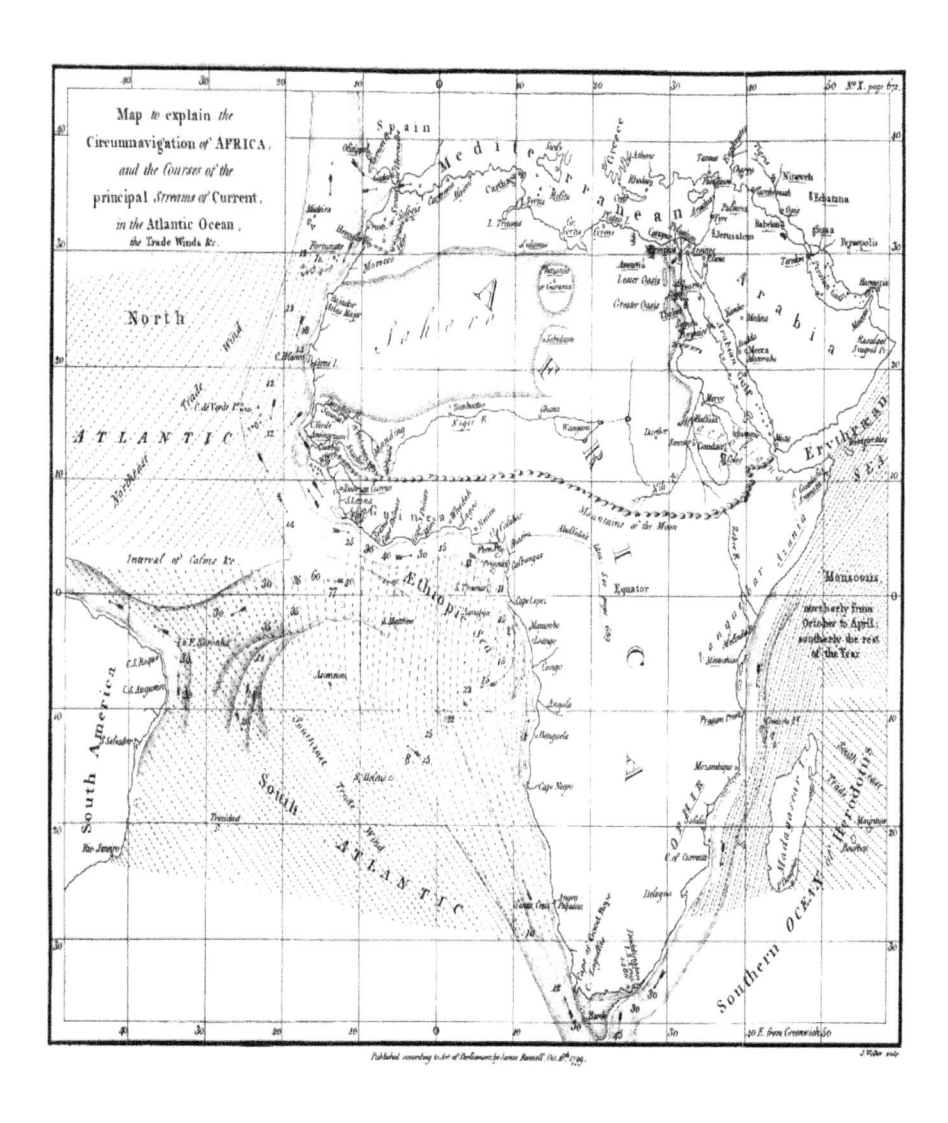

125 | *Tales From The City State Of Ophir*

Malachy Postlethwayte 1755 map Southern Africa

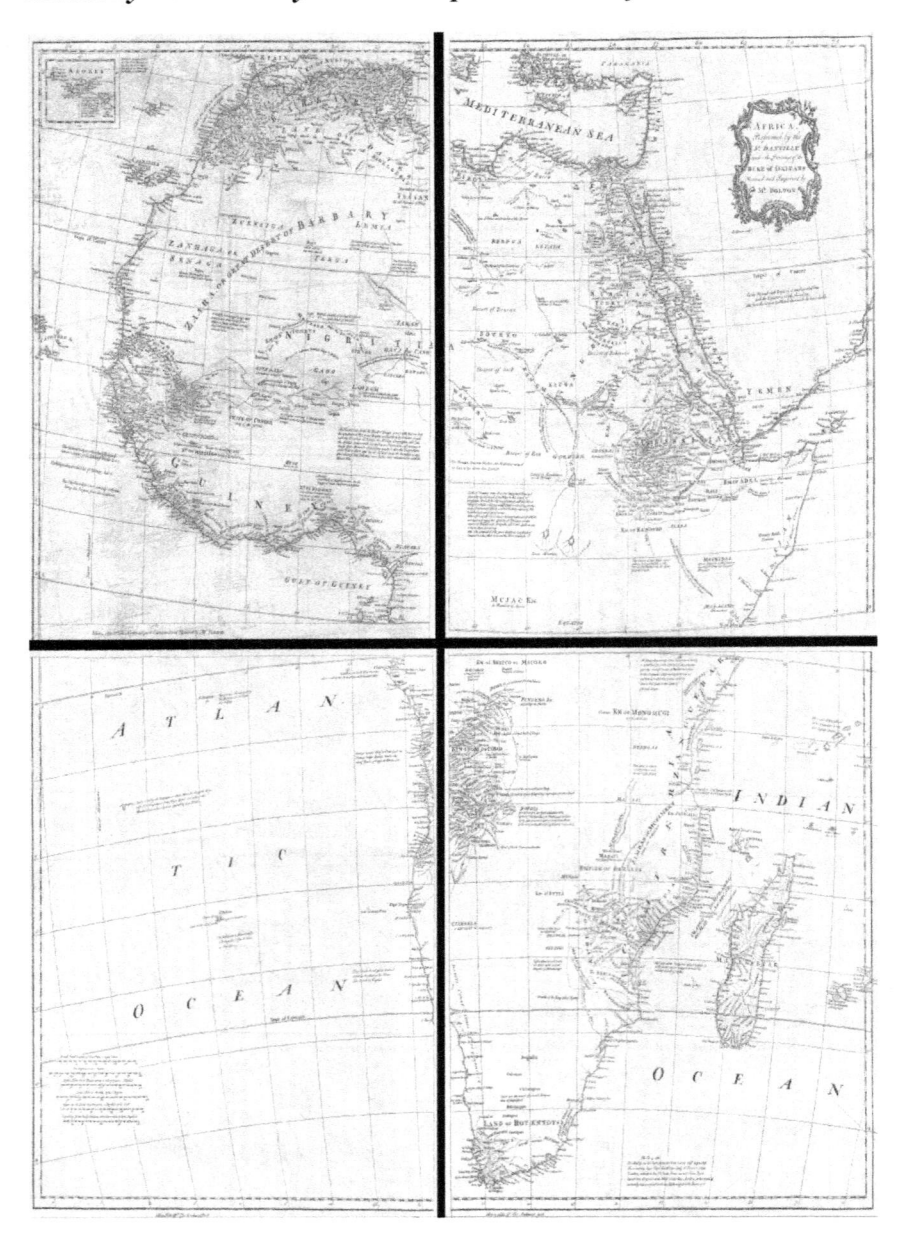

Malachy Postlethwayte 1755 map zoomed in

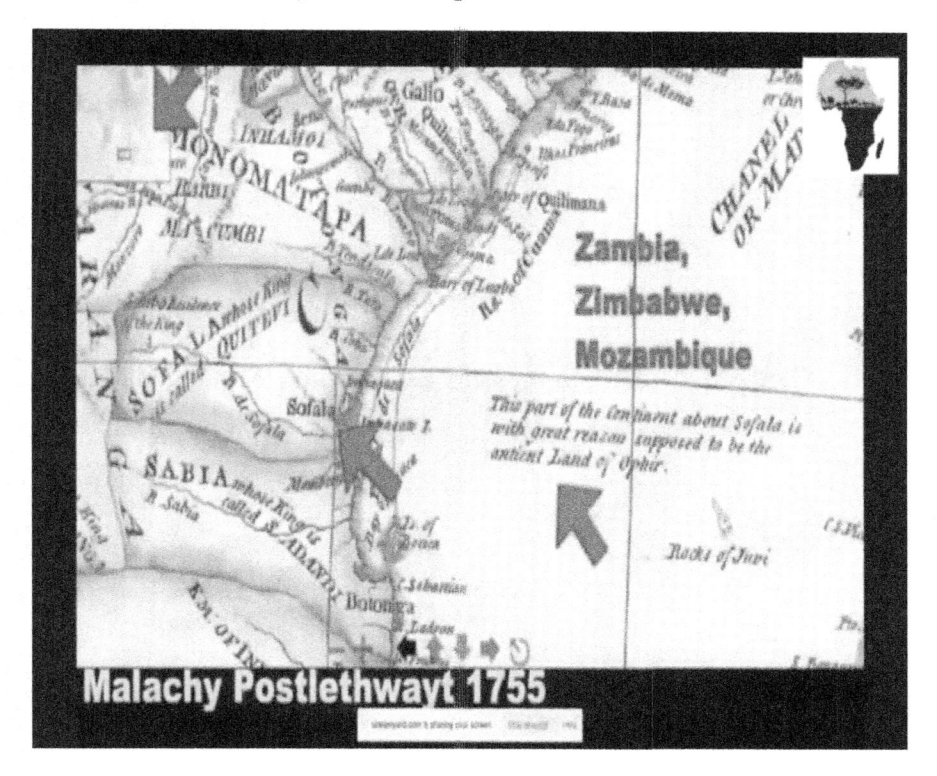

2 Esdras 6:9 KJV 1611

"For Esau is the end of the world, and Yakobe is the beginning of it that followeth." (Prepare yourselves Bantwanawami!)

127 | *Tales From The City State Of Ophir*

Written for kingdom Press by C. Mpumelelo Mängenä

Printed in Great Britain
by Amazon